LOST HORSE PRESS NEW POETS SERIES

New Poets | *Short Books*

ACTS OF CONTRITION

THE OWL'S EARS

LIMINAL: A LIFE OF CLEAVAGE

To Audrey —
I hope all of your
poetic whims and
dreams come true :

LOST HORSE PRESS NEW POETS SERIES

New Poets | *Short Books*
Series Editor | Marvin Bell

ACTS OF CONTRITION

Gwendolyn Cash

THE OWL'S EARS

Boyd W. Benson

LIMINAL: A LIFE OF CLEAVAGE

Lisa Galloway

LOST HORSE PRESS
SANDPOINT • IDAHO

Acknowledgments

Gwendolyn Cash
Birmingham Poetry Review: "Your Palm Pressed to Mine"
Cutthroat: "Mirror"

Boyd Benson
The Iowa Review: "Saving One's Self a Lot of Grief"

Lisa Galloway
Perigee: "She Was a Chagall"
"Signs" and "Acquisition vs. Creation" previously
appeared in a collaborative chapbook titled, *Paint.*

FIRST EDITION

Book design by Christine Holbert
Gwendolyn Cash photo by John Campbell
Boyd W. Benson photo by Terri Benson
Lisa Galloway photo by Elizabeth A. Oliver

Library of Congress Cataloging-in-Publication Data

Cash, Gwendolyn, 1968-
  Acts of contrition / Gwendolyn Cash. The owl's ears / Boyd W.
Benson. Liminal : a life of cleavage / Lisa Galloway.
      p. cm.—(Lost Horse Press new poets series. New poets, short
books)
  ISBN 978-0-9762114-7-1 (alk. paper)
  1. American poetry-—21st century. I. Benson, Boyd W., 1961-
II. Galloway, Lisa, 1978- III. Title. IV. Title: Owl's ears. V. Title:
Liminal.
  PS617.C37 2007
  811'.608--dc22
                    2006100084

The idea for this series is indebted to *Poets of Today,* the Scribner series edited by John Hall Wheelock from 1954 to 1962, which published in eight volumes first books by twenty-four poets, three poets at a time under a single cover. There were fewer of us then. A poet who received the good fortune of book publication would forever thereafter be accorded the status of a serious writer.

Forty-five years later, the competition to publish a first book of poetry is ferocious. Nor does a first book, given the number that appear annually, serve now to define one's commitment to the art. If one does not "network" (that ugly verb) in the centers of literary opinion, or write with a bow to theory or fashion, it can be more difficult yet. The mechanism of book contests, while mostly honorable, is also dispiriting.

The increased promotion in recent years of American poetry on many levels owes much to a dumbing-down of the art and the proliferation of novelty acts. Yet the country is also chock-full of little-published poets of higher seriousness.

This 3-in-1 series, then, is intended to sample a range of poets who have yet to publish a book and have generally gone about their writing in private. It will not be run as a contest, nor will it accept submissions. The usual biographical notes will be replaced by brief personal statements. Its covers will not carry promotional blurbs.

I believe that, in the matter of poetry, two heads are half as good as one. Therefore, the poems in these short books will be selected and arranged by their authors with minimal editorial interference. The poets will not be asked to adjust their poetry to a house style.

I hope that these samplings, presented with as few trappings as possible, will reaffirm for readers the nature of the *poetry* in poetry. Serious poetry is not written to satisfy literary opinion. Poetry, like philosophy, is a survival skill.

M.B

Table of Contents

Liminal: A Life of Cleavage | LISA GALLOWAY

ACTS *of* CONTRITION

poems | GWENDOLYN CASH

Gwendolyn Cash

I was born in 1968 in Spokane and have lived in the state of Washington all my life. That, and poetry, have been two of the few anchors in my life. I fell in love with poetry as a student when a Presbyterian minister smuggled a copy of Carolyn Forché's *The Country Between Us* into my backpack at a retreat. I am preoccupied with recording in poetry the worlds of ordinary people, the things that make me love and hate them, and the things I don't understand. In writing, I am an external recorder of human behavior and emotion and, in moments of self loathing and pity, an internal critic.

Today, I'm going to lie about everything. I'm going to lie about what I learned at school. I'm going to lie about calculus because I stopped at geometry even though I shouldn't have, even though I have a deep affection, a love, raw and pure, for mathematics, but that could be another lie. I'm going to lie about what happens in alleyways and parking lots and at the end of dark roads, the thefts, the beatings, the forced entries, the blood, piss, and semen puddled in the good rain, but I think these truths have shifted to the right, perhaps, and my lies will make things easier in the way lilies make grief something we can bear. I'm going to lie about brushing my teeth and what's in the mailbox because no one wants to trace a family's shame in its choleric path into the trash and the sewer, and even if some fool did, it's not a story that can be told in realities, if there ever was such. I'm going to lie about my shoe size to keep up appearances and lie about headaches and books to make a good impression. I'm going to lie about how many times I let a man break my heart, how many times I looked in his eyes hoping for a piece of myself, and finding nothing, crawled into the animal warmth of his body, gambling against the time when there was nothing left to take or give. I'm going to lie about every time I went back and begged him to break me again. I'm going to lie on the sidewalk, on the train, and in my own home, my sanctuary of toothpicks and white glue, mashed potatoes and grilled lamb, sweet spices, and a cello faintly mourning. I'm going to lie with my hands on the wheel when I merge. I'm going to lie locked in the little wooden box at Confession. I haven't been there in years, but Father, yes, Father? Forgive you and your sin. I'm going to lie when I button my jeans, lie about how much I am wont to think about my skin and everything inside it, this indulgence embodied in the downy flesh on my belly stung by metal rivets hot from the dryer. I'm going to lie in my own music, lie in the shower, and lie in every goddamned cup of tea I drink. I'm going to lie when I smile and smile when I lie. I'm going to lie when you smile. I'm going to lie to you. I'm going to look in the mirror and lie about time and everything called true: that I am cracked, bent, and broken, that I feel pain that has no words, that I hate where life has dropped me for the day, and that I love nothing more today than all these precious fucking little lies.

Suppose that god of yours
is sleeping.

Suppose no serpent
shudders behind your heel.

Suppose you have made
your own hell.

Something surfaces
in the brackish water, bobs
toward your waiting fingers, a gold
fruit recovered from the flood.

Suppose it is not forbidden.

Suppose you take it
with these naked hands,
rub its fragrance
into your skin, break it
open and breathe
for the first time into its flesh.

Suppose you suck
the juices over your lips,
force your tongue
into the pulp and close
your eyes.

Suppose you find
the rough touch of the gnarled pit,
the heart's stony genesis.

You could sin
that deeply. You could
be mortal like the peaches
in the rainswept orchard, fallen
and bruised. You could
feel something more
beautiful, more terrifying
than need.

All pieces can be
cut into smaller
pieces, and when
there isn't quite
enough, it is
a fact of the kitchen—
if you mince a little
more, you create
an illusion of
abundance. Things
stretch further.
Salt adds flavor
and pickles flesh.
Add a measure
of milk, a splash
of wine or spirits,
you have art.
On the chopping
block, in the fire,
you might conjure
enough to go
around. Forget
the fractures,
the disembodiments,
the pulverizing,
and bruising. Forget
genius soaked
in sauce, crusted
in grit and ash.
In the end,
nothing comes

to the table without
bleeding, without
losing something,
does it?

Acts of Contrition

Dear Forgiveness, you know that recently
we have had our difficulties and there are many things
I want to ask you.

"Litany in Which Certain Things are Crossed Out"
—Richard Siken

I

Because I was born, every morning will be a ritual cleansing,
  each waking an effort to construct a melody that can be
    recorded, transcripted in treble and bass, something
      that makes sense.
This will unravel, somehow, somewhere in between.
                         Lost every morning,
the verses, the chorus, the ornamentations just another jingle,
another scam hawking love,
  preaching the shoulds and should nots
    Because I gave you life, you are born to fail and die.
Maybe I wanted to thwart you,
               to ring your little prophecy by the neck.
                  Maybe I wanted
to give you something more than a pretty list,
  accomplishments to fashion into a pasteboard crown,
    fungal benevolence growing in the trash.
                   Maybe I did.
Yes, I have always been this desperate.
  Mother, I'm sorry for staying away so long.
        Mother, I woke up one day and you said
  I wish you could have made something of your life.
        The wish is granted. I did it. Mother, I'm sorry.

II

But I'm not. Poor mother.
   You wanted to make something of me. Everyone does.
I have painted myself in flowers,
     slept under cypresses hung in moss. I have grown a heart
      that cleaves to the moon. It never sleeps.
              But, you say, *it will never be enough.*
So drown me in a lily pond, then. Hang me in a maple
   in the dead of winter.
     I'll play in the trees, play a little piano, play a little
      nocturne for you at midday in A minor,
        a requiem, an elegy tremulous, oh, so sad . . .
Oh, come celebrate my joyous birth, my coming,
   my opening to this world. Oh, lost and brilliant girl, tender
     girl I was,
     like every tender girl, sweet music. Oh, but shame . . .
                I've roused the devil.
Something naughty is creeping into the melodies
   on the black and white keys,
too quick, too hot, too many notes. Only a witch
   could conjure this.
                Or a whore.

III

You think I'm the devil. I know this.
   It would be just like me to be something I'm not,
                you think, to aspire
to terrible greatness. You think, but you're wrong.
   I'm not the devil. I'm not the blessed virgin either.
             I'm a woman.
I write things. Terrible things.
             I touch things. Touch people.
Every day, I trample your dreams, and in the rubbish,

I find a broken crystal ball. I see a shattered future.
  I shun duty. I suffocate your plastic love, and true,
    I drink poison and laugh about it,
                                but not right now.
That day when you pinned me to the wall, I screamed,
  spitting blood,
    I love you less than the cat,
                      and your face white, I said
    I am as dead to you as you want me to be.
                      Be good now.
                                We'll get there soon.

I thought I was the devil once.
  I am not afraid of it now. I thought I was
    coated in sugared ice, glowing like an aurora, waiting,
locked in my room, waiting,
              a pair of blue eyes staring from a window,
                      just a girl, not beautiful,
frozen in time and temperament, thawing a bloodless heart
  over a fire,
    no love to burn, waiting for something to catch,
to take away the pick-axe cold, something like love,
  but I didn't trust the signs,
    didn't know what to look for on my watch
  for love on a white horse,
                      a black horse,
  love crossing in high runoff,
                      love pulling me under the ice,
  love in flames,
                      love bleeding in a bathroom sink.

IV

Maybe I am the devil. Get over it.
  You're still the chosen one with a book of rules,

the magic wand, and eyes shooting bullets. Your tongue
     spreads poison and lies, lies, and lies.
                    An alchemist, an amateur,
you sealed hope eternally in a cobwebbed jar
                    and left it on the highest shelf.
Forty years adrift, but any minute now, I will be sixteen again.
   I will pretend you're really here
                    because it's Saturday night again.
The telephone is ringing, and neither of us are here
   in my room, on my bed
                    as you cut off all my hair.
Our skin smells of violets. Your own hair, like wire,
   is impossibly coarse, so it follows
                         that mine must go.
                    I say *no*. But maybe *no*
is something you cannot hear. Some would say so,
   but of these, we must not speak.

I had the dream last night where you spin
   straw and poverty into gold
                    before you kill my father,
   who carved the charmed spindle
                    for your pleasure.

V

I wish, Mother, I could have done it right once,
   for the newspapers, knocked 'em cold, caught the big one,
      brought home the gold in my hands,
                         hung it on your neck
and sent you off to heaven.
   Wouldn't that have been something.
I kept a few secrets, you know, kept them hidden
   in my father's armor,
covered my victor's bruises in long sleeves and powder,

released the speckled trout.
A wicked tongue inside your head whispers
  and chortles when you try to hear the words,
    the actual words,
      not just their ghosts echoing in your head
        where you kill them to make them your own.
You reach in a dresser, pick up the gun
  and you're off and running,
    running into the back yard on Easter Sunday, running,
your kid gloves leaving no prints,
  around and around you go in Italian pumps,
    finger on the trigger,
                    I wonder what stopped you.
You're still here? Then I'm sorry. Sorry I don't look as much
  like you as you thought, legs too short, lips too full,
sorry I had to ask you, pester you, beg you for so much,
  to tax you into debt, love debts so deep
    you've put yourself in prison, sorry for the betrayals,
the writing, the cocksure philosophies, the heathen children,
  my deep affection for them,
                    my deep affection for them,
sorry I made you cry,
  sorry I put it down for the record.
                    I'm sorry.
  I am everything you say I am.

VI

Mother, I must confess my habit I picked up
  somewhere of breaking everything into pieces.
    I carry them in a velvet bag into my cave
      where in firelight
                I can see
how they were formed, why they are heft and lightness
  in my hands as they are.

It's all true.
I like to see fire glittering on a fractured plane.
  Listen, for once,
              I'm not like you,
squeezing out the last breaths, wringing out the blood.
I put them back together.
                    I swear.
Sometimes things are different when I am done.
  I can't help it. Sometimes you hold me silently.
You stroke my long hair, curling it around your finger
  in the lamplight. You don't think of scissors.
    You love the smell of me,
        bitter salt scalp, milky breath,
          the sound of me,
    the ocean in a pulse against your ear. You gaze at me,
                eyes soft for once, and see the pale child I was,
    as I see my own I hold to my breast,
      true pearls, uncultured and raw.
No grades, no disappointments.
  No performances. No recitals with a case of nerves
    and no breakfast.
      Starvation quells that kind of hunger.
It is easier this way, this different way of remembering,
  and for this, I could take it all back.
      the blind hedges and dead ends of your mind,
      another hospital, more chrysanthemums, red lipstick,
      the goddamned violets,
  I take it all back.

VII

You know I am lying. I do, too, because I can't now,
  take it back. You wouldn't either.
But if you think you have done it all for me,
  if you think I have failed,

if you think you can do it better,
then it is time, time for your paper, your pencil,
   time for your pile of rubbish and aphorisms,
      time to manufacture histories with a pen
                        and a bucket of blood and tears.
If the sun shines on your face, you are in our brittle house.
If the sun shines on your heart,
   and it is making you warm,
      making you wonder,
                        then we are getting somewhere.
But if the sun shines and you say it does,
   I will know you are lying.
Conjure yourself a temple, goddess, with pencil and paper.
                        Call this Folly.
Conjure me a crypt, witch, and I will call it Forgiveness.
Yes, we have been there, Mother.
   You said you knew the way, and I believed.
      The treasure was already stolen, though
                  the coffers emptied. So do it again.
Build me a sanctuary,
   the walls painted hospital-white, the door knobs gleaming.
Bring me rice pudding with raisins
   and one last slice of buttered sourdough toast.
The chemistry of love can be explained like rising bread,
   with examples and admonitions.

VIII

We are out of time, Mother.
   Forget the devil,
   leave the gun in the drawer.
                  This has nothing to do with love.
This is the place where we live as you desire,
   luscious and golden in our old house,
      standing in the doorframe

of your fragrant kitchen,
                    your fingers pressing into my arms,
into the soft skin on my neck.
  Your thumbs are squeezing as I say
    I am as dead to you as you ever wanted me to be.
    You hate that ending, the crying, the choking,
so write your own. I never wanted to tell you
                                    you were wrong.
It's your turn. You hesitate and pout. This disgusts me.
  Do you see now? It takes more
    than a promise, more than a bonfire,
      more than guns and pills.
        Your remedies don't work.
                          But I have not forgotten
croquet in the back yard in summer dresses,
  walks on empty beaches,
    and hot tea and milk on a few winter mornings.
Call it love, call it responsibility,
                    call it your god-damned sacrifice,
                              take your pick.
I can't do any better than this.

IX

I am building a fire
  on the image of innocence between us.
      Blessed be your angry heels tapping up the steps.
      Blessed be your haphazard mascara.
      Blessed be the water glass ringed in minerals
        by your lonely bed.
      Blessed be those who love us and those who love
        against us.
Thanks be for the happy faces smiling at the camera,
  greedy for bounty and forgiveness.
Thanks be that our hands are joined, our eyes closed.

We are blessed amongst women.
                         None of us deserve it.

X

In darkness, a ghost kitchen, a phantom yard, spirits sobbing
    in the closet.
A river of headlights streamed past my window every night
    while I waited for my father's truck in the drive.
I am watching you sleep, Mother, as I promised,
    watching a wicked tongue whispering in your ear,
        and when you wake up
            and try to hear the words, it will be me again,
                                    the blessed devil,
                showing you a goldfinch on your sill.
It has been five minutes since these words appeared
    on the page,
        five minutes since I started a fire,
            but I doubt I can conjure enough warmth to save us.
The pictures curl into themselves,
                    the words float around us in ashes.
                                    Then darkness.
                We are as dim and misunderstood as death,
    but I can't expect you to embrace this. You are so tuned
        to the voice
            whispering in your head,
                the devil's voice assuring you that yes,
the goldfinch has chosen you, as we all had to choose you,
    that he has chosen this life, this window,
        because you understand him,
            because you are benevolent,
                because sometimes,
                    the devil is impossibly kind.

Bully

You ought to spit on his shoes, kick him
in the balls; instead, you pick up
the books you dropped,
and walk away, spine and neck
anchored in pride as your eyes blink back
from the tops of your patent leather shoes.
No matter the scrape on your knee
or the ripped hem of your dress.
What burns deeper than pain or shame
is the hate you never let go, your own
creation you coddle and stoke
every breathing minute,
but twenty years later, you will stand in line
at a post office and see his picture
on the wall. You'll catch a glimpse
of his face on the news,
the scene electrified in flashing
red and blue lights.
You will be teaching in a prison
when he shuffles through the door,
a broken, used-up mule.
Your eyes will deepen, your skin
will lose its blush. Shaking,
you'll hand him a sheet of paper
and a sharpened pencil, your throat
so dry it hurts, saying,
Tell me your story.
Tell it like it is.

Anesthesiologist

Come to us in our gowns
thin and shabby,
shadows ringing our eyes,
scared weary as we wait for the wound,
to be cut open, splayed by gloved hands,
and picked apart, the surgeon's upper lip
sweating under the lights.
We will bleed,
be clamped and stitched,
never the same as before.

Give us the antidote
for pain,
            for memory,
the needle's smooth slide
into the skin,
full of promises.

Our lids droop, tongues
whisper
buried secrets,
            how we forged
our mothers' signatures when we failed
geometry, how we only like the icing
on German chocolate cake, how I loved
a man like a brother,
but I'm sorry,
I fucked him instead,
how a blind man remembers
the color of an orange.

I hold your hand, demi-god.
Your cold nectar swims in my veins,
a siren song of nothingness.
Sweet nothings
                    I whisper
Give me more.

We're drinking whiskey with our eggs.
He's been rolling asphalt all night.
I rolled joints and drank cheap wine
on the tailgate of his Chevy.
He tells good stories.

Tell me about Monique and Veronica,
women whose names are tattooed
on each side of his brown neck.
I like to trace them with my finger.
You can't tell a lady a story like that,
he grins and orders two more drinks.

I know he is going to leave me,
but at 6 AM in the Brown Derby
drinking it neat with my toast,
I don't care,
and my body believes
the biggest lies of all
when he points
to a fresh mermaid on his shoulder
touches my face with his hardened hand—

Have I told you
how I walked through a desert
so thirsty my tongue fell asleep
dreaming of a river in the saguaro,
and when I crossed the ditch at Juarez,
I was still in that same river
and when I saw you
two thousand miles upstream

diving from the rocks, I knew
I was in the same deep water as you —
the same deep water as you.

In the Mirror

This is what I am in love,
Grandmother, a pouting face
in the mirror, looking back
into yours, eyeliner reflected
on a blue iris, rouged cheeks,
red lipstick waiting to rub off
on a collar, a mouth. Grandmother,
I want to buy you a drink tonight,
gin and tonic with two limes.
I will lick my lips, touch his thigh,
and eat cake off someone's fork.
In the mirror over my shoulder,
you watch from your photograph,
hair bobbed, crimped with feathers,
nails lacquered dark, arms bare.
Loose woman, your shoulders curve
as mine, identically toned and slack.
We wear black stockings, smooth
coolness fitted to warm flesh,
the ridged seam stretched from painted toes,
across the foot's tender arch and calf,
up the thigh to the lace at the top
where a satin garter, with pink silk rosettes,
tugs against gravity and the inevitable
slide to the floor in a silken puddle
on a pair of velvet heels.
Bad girl, tart, tawdry woman,
love without shame. Look at me.
I will take you to bed with me.

Bluegrass

Last night on the back porch
I swam the river past the junked cars
and the welfare office,
the precious ladies at the church
with their hats and mean mouths,
past my mother with her vague smile,
sorting buttons into jars and tiny
cardboard boxes, waving at my daughters
turning leggy cartwheels in the watery sun,
past my son crouched in the dust
under the tree, waiting for the animal
to show its face in the hole just once,
past a husband whistling,
whittling something out of nothing
for better or for worse. I drifted
past girls at sixteen smoking
by the dumpster behind the Conoco,
past a bikini-sunburned picnic
at Diamond Lake and first kisses,
first sex on someone's couch in the afternoon
after school before a father came home
covered in road grime, looking for cold water
and beer, past a lost baby, a pearl
glistening in the sand, and there
I found an eddy and waited
for my father to come out of a thicket
calling my name,
his pockets full of something
like blackberries and forget-me-nots.
He offered the best ones to the oldest
woman and gave me the rest,
asking me to follow around the bend,

and I went because of his smile,
his tanned forearms, his blue eyes.
By then he was treading water.
We all were.
Even after the water flowed away
into the ocean and the stones bleached
white in the sun, we swam the night river,
laughing, all the daughters and fathers,
the sons, wives, brothers,
the favorite aunts heading home again
into the dim light on the horizon.

THE OWL'S EARS

poems | BOYD W. BENSON

Boyd W. Benson

In my heart there is a little old lady. A spinster, actually. Each night as spiders spin shadows through the corners of a room, she stays up late. She listens to the door and crochets pillowcases. Deep down, though, she's as wild as the sparrowgrass. I write poems to keep a far-off look in her eye, to keep her whistling (even though, I'm sure, she'd much prefer the company of Emily Dickenson). A lifelong Washingtonian, I was born in Seattle in 1961 and grew up in Everett and on Whidbey Island. I (and the little old lady in my heart) now live with my wife, Terri, three fine stepsons, and two Chihuahuas in Clarkston, Washington, above the Snake River, where the sparrowgrass whistles.

Saving One's Self a Lot of Grief

I hoard in a small box,
decorative, yet not too

loud, those old sorrows,
those true companions.

Unlike the old barber
whose griefs will bellow

like many mangy dogs,
my griefs are brilliant

singers and so delicate.
They are small things,

fine as spiders' webbing,
and quite mesmerizing.

I press them into my box,
gently, one atop the other.

They spring back to my touch.
It is an elegant, clever system.

Unlike the sorrows of others,
which tend to tire the mind

too easily, you will appreciate
and marvel so at my griefs

you will grieve yourself
for not having them.

I will not be letting them go.

It Was Too Late

I never saw myself coming.
The simple eyes of storeroom clerks
did not see me. And local dogs
lay down with the sound of my name.

I was that problematic.
A cheeseburger beneath a glass
umbrella. A dusty tube radio
signaling nothing.

There were many tall trees
and likewise crow obscenities
beneath them. I did not
stop. They did not see me.

I did not see myself in others,
the boozy young army reservists
or the old women of silken bones.
I could not remember dreams.

That day reached around me
with the laziness of grass,
a whim to the incalculable stars
set deep within their history.

Someone made a hat and tossed it in the air,
a new motto waved a flag, and the shadows
spoke freely without us. It was a dictum
could make a heart shine like a small star
and a mouth feel the song in it.
Then someone threw a parade and marched
the bones home, regiment by regiment.

First, the white thumb-bones of buglers,
then the thighbones of boys named Andy or Bill.
It was a beautiful hollow sound the bones made.
Too beautiful for us. Nobody cared to listen.
One man played Taps and it had a jazzy
new snap to it. O we could throw a parade
in those days. We could make a fine hat.

While You Were Gone

I didn't plan the milk to turn lumpish.
The black bouquet delivered to your door,
didn't intend that either.

The blindfolded swan in the bathtub.
The seven boiled starlings in the kitchen.
The jawbone of the landlord tied to a string.

I only wanted your undivided attention
before the shadows vanished with you.
The hippopotamus was a complete accident.

Today I am watching the circles
squirrels cut around the elm.
I am tracing the sun's path, and then
a moth's furious orbit around the lamp.

I am considering the amplitude of zero,
where the enclosure of nothing
meets itself and returns home
carrying a horizon on its back.

Today I am watching the old horse
slant her long nose to the ground,
her lengthy back a crescent,
sort of wisdom, too.

Owl

Some say it flies backwards.
A species of amusing thought,

an idea flying through trees,
late at night, its large eyes

glimpsing what it just missed,
then, shut tight, envisioning a future.

The Opener of Doors

It begins with a slight ache,
a pulse or a throb underfoot,
the weight of the sky upon it.
The grass suffers.
Stones dig deep within themselves,
beneath other stones,
where water makes waves
and disappears
and cloudburst fizzles into steam.
Where even God suffers,
the fever that becomes humankind
leads to a solitary man
darting through the trees,
over hills and ridges.

In the chapels, over the half-emptied glass,
in the kiss of carlights on distant roads,
his face is that of the weather
or a field of lilies—or an apple orchard.
And he runs, the opener of doors,
across the fields, his eyes like glass,
breath metallic moist,
he who heaps stones in small piles
and crosses cabin floors,
unscrewing the lightbulbs of poor farmers.
As cities rise in a cluster from the plains,
cling to doze on a shrinking horizon,
he sleeps in a hole he digs himself
beneath a blanket of dew.

Where Quasimodo rings the bell,
he runs the rim of valleys,

a shadow among shadows,
a pure ringing in the trees.
He's cultivated the yellow mask
of the moon
and fashioned the blaze of the sun
into many small jewels.
He's wrenched the wallpaper
from the wall
and broken the shovel
on the stone,
the stone on his teeth
with his ear to the cold.

He's loosed the screw
on the wheelchair.
And taken a hammer
to the portrait of a mother.

In a field of triangles,
he's drawn a circle
and in the circle
a door.

He stands outside the circle.

The Janitors Next Door

They are sweeping and polishing a zero
from door to door, a city block of zeros.
They are circling the dust and opening doors,
perfuming the impossible behind the dark
windows of storefronts. It is night,
always night—the exquisite alcohol
moon. They sweep up what's left
of our lives, the surplus of us—
misplaced letters, black threads,
the sawdust off our shoes.

I hear them in the basement at night,
sighing and stumbling
through my life in a thorny way,
a pile of teeth in a dustpan,
a mound of fingernails, bad memories
I thought I'd forgotton
stuffed in a large garbage bag.
They are pushing the zero
across the floor, propping it up
next to their godliness.
Hidee hi, hidee ho! They are dealing
a hand of seven-card flush.

Rake

An orphan's smile
is all spindle and rut.

Air between the teeth
fresh as spider's breath.

The extended throat
for dark fruit.

The Silent Comedians

Look for them in the thistles,
behind rusty keyholes,
in the sleep of lions and lilies,
in snow and ice,
in the footprints of the ocean.

Look for them
in plush velvet cloakrooms,
in the dark corners
of a room, in the green hours
before sex.

They have clutched their hands
into fists and blossomed
into flowers, weeds and hills,
in fields of grain, beneath the pantomime
of clouds.

They sit behind a glass of water,
where they've closed their eyes
to become the shape of prayer,
the yawn of sunset and the flat surface
of mirrors.

They wave to you with frail hands
and the helpless logic of gravel,
from the vertebrae of pigs,
a polished bullet clamped between the teeth,
in the idiot hours before dawn.

The Owl's Ears

I've known the shadows to sweep
over a day, at dusk, down the stairs,
one at a time, silence like that,

the singing of hands,
the conversation of skin,
a fountain pen and dying light.

Then, the owl's ears grow larger
for such music the trees bring,
and the shadows that sweep

a glass coated with dust,
of course, grow larger, too.
Yes, a certain sort of dignity

can never be diminished
as it climbs down steps,
one at a time, and is gone.

The Schoolyard

Then, I wept with the clock,
always presently more
afterward than before

moss grew on each savage
hand. Nails had loosened
from the architecture

of my skull, like a finger
in a bicycle wheel:
I was a bad amigo.

You carried a map
of yourself and pointed
shyly to each county line,

coal mining country,
the backbone of industry,
and to the flashlight on your hat.

A mouse began to spin
from door to door
across the schoolyard

as we estimated how many
Toodaloos it might take
to get us somewhere.

Hats

Some are brimmed to consider the sky,
to keep sun from our eyes or funnel rain.
Some wool ones we've designed only
to contain a head,
a place to hide the cold abstraction.
We wear a tasseled hat to graduate
into the world and throw it toward the sun,
and many hats after
can land on an unsuspecting head.
One small hat has a black veil for death.
Another means you're a bride.
A top hat helped Fred Astaire climb stairs
with grace, or danced in his hand
while descending.
A tip of it can mean good day, good-bye.
A rabbit out of it and you're a magician.
(And nobody frowns at a hat trick.)
One hat deflects a curveball, another a bullet
from the brain.
One man wears a hat for every day,
and though we might not
trust him, we admire him just the same.
Merlin wore the entire universe on his head.

Middle Name

Rarely repeated, seldom heard,
the secret hub of you.

Squeezed between the lips
of public identity

the flower's core. You didn't pick it.
It grew before you

turned your head, the first time,
to the others.

Light

The air softens,

behind the blue
of a swan's neck,

on my skin
like the shadow

the starling leaves
behind,

as through branches
of a burnished oak

or polished water
or steam

where night is always
falling.

Morning sprinklers
begin to hiss

and barking dogs echo
down the streets

the wild unintelligible
we exist.

One always stands on the wrong side,
opens it, walks out, only to want back in.

One door opens the stale mouth of old clothes.
One to the milky white of a coughing lung.

One door exposes a birch with black branches,
a crow's yellow eye gazing back.

As always with great liberators
so intolerably oppressive like this,

one door hides behind another.
You never see it until too late.

To the Nursing Home Escapee Karl G.

After the sun slips past these rooftops into night,
you should wrap yourself in the sky left behind.
Where yesterday a green hummingbird,
size of your thumb, suckled red begonias,
you should wander the streets now like your own
    lost lover.
You should stand at the corner of your choosing,
search the air for any sign of sweetness or alarm.

Then recall the light of this streetlamp
after the last of you has left you here—
seated tonight, by the last window of the last bus,
after the silence departs, and you have wandered off—

and the many white winged moths that shone beneath.

When he let himself go,
the milkweed still grew.

Flowers augmented dirt
to grow many tiny eyes
open wide to the sky

when he abandoned all hope.

Someone said they saw him on a bus.
Someone else said, oh.

Someone said what he had said,
only different.

The cafes closed at night,
bees flew crazy figures on the air
while he fingered his beard,

watching boats fall off the horizon.

Review

Did I say the owl that circles its own sleep
like a cloud is not a bird but a fever,
a blaze of weather, a thunderbolt of feathers
and the skin of the fallen sky in a rain of ash?

Did I mention the trembling bee,
the apple of my eye, the quivering wing
of raw honey, cultivates its yellow
from lightbulbs and the moon?

Of course, too many things go unsaid
soar like this, from morning to night, small things
we catch in sleep or witness in a fervor,
holding no more than a sky over our heads.

I should point out, too, the black ocean
behind the mask of sleep lacks wings,
and so has soaked and sunk into itself
the dark gravity of its own understanding.

To the Moments after Midnight Rain

Each drop
a chime,
a small glass
bell
circling itself,
a map
for lost days
is how I find it,
where X marks
the impossible,
and even crickets
are listening.

Each drop
a possible ocean
spilling in waves
on foreign shores
and a probable cause
for the ears of old women,
the aloofness of clouds,
a gesture
of blue distance held near,
of the closeness of wet stones
to our lives,
of lives balanced
between the stars,
carried on the glossy back of a bird
and the blood-leak of trees.

I have seen the light
in the raindrop
magnify the horizon

like an eye wide open,
where the horn of a bull
in an unfamiliar terrain
slashes air
and a rose falls from the sky,
where the bows of schooners
slice the surge beneath their sails,
which is the water of men's lives,
the sweet milk
of human forgiveness,
where a man can drown
beneath something like happiness,
or a shower of stars,
or the countless lights of a far off city.

I have plotted the luminosity
of the raindrop
to fall at exact angles,
at precise times.
To know its small glow
burst on my cheek.

When a gray
bucket catches it,
the raindrop
becomes moonlight,
a ripple,
a shadow,
a dwelling for street light
or a face
behind the ghost
of a man,
a bucket of blood,
a dripping Christ,
transubstantiation

of galvanized steel
and cloud work
expanding to its limit
and back,
where a sky can reflect
and be held.

When I was a boy
rain swirled
into galaxies
beneath black rubber galoshes
and made windshields cry.
Beneath rain's radiance,
graves looked greener.
Beneath rain,
the air said autumn.

LIMINAL: A LIFE OF CLEAVAGE

poems | LISA GALLOWAY

Lisa Galloway

Good poetry like whiskey writhes, romances, and with white-knuckled fists fights the within out of. Human nature, that is, peoples' psychological impulses interest me far more than trees or birds, mostly because I think poetry should be a shock to the senses, it should evoke something and it should leave you with something, and for me the crazy things that people do is where it's at. I was born in Indianapolis, Indiana on April 24, 1978, adopted nine days later to grow up an-hour-of-cornfield-north in Kokomo, Indiana. No, not the Kokomo from the Beach Boys song, the winters are cold with too much snow, which is one of the many reasons that I moved to Portland, Oregon in June of 2005.

The worst part is the way you are stuck
in a 7th grade, black and white drawing
on perspective, the one where
the vanishing point is all askew
and the lines marked too hard
against the ruler have been erased
over and again, so that you aren't sure
where buildings or sidewalks
begin and end, and like you
are in Plato's cave chained,
you can't turn around to see
that the road does go on,
and there is more to life than shadows,
even though the buildings
are all wrong angles.

Sometimes you stay
because you're still searching
for the words that should have been
her suicide note.
You don't want to repeat
or hear one more time "like mother, like daughter,"
you have to stay while your brain god
keeps splitting your world in two,
dividing you down the middle into
tolerant oblivion, just a slow motion ride
because you gave up trying just before
she blew her punch line, but wake up, because someone
will have to go out for cigarettes soon.

Axiom of Ontology

I imagine you all day
at work flitting with wings, your little body
against his light
until he removes the glass,
and I think:
I'm always gathering her up in my arms
like newspapers or dirty clothes
from my floor, trying to hold, trying to place her,
eventually the glass will get too hot
from the flame burning crooked,
and it will shatter and splay,
pinning a moment to a board
for the purpose of nomenclature
to study and name the iridescence of wings.
And when this happens,
I won't be there,
but I may come later to talk at you,
opening the drawer to pull out the shadow box
that you are pinned inside of, and
I'll finally get it then, we are not the same species,
though our lives wouldn't have been much different
than this either way.
I don't know love, but I think it is like pulling out
what you think is an empty drawer
and finding things that hold your interest.
What doesn't begin this way and end in death
with memories pinned against your loneliness?

Our Worlds in Collision

The black and blue flowers on my bedroom wall
always baffled me, but I suppose they are a great metaphor.

I was five when we moved in,
and, Dad, you were all blowtorch
and putty knife,
one plank at a time,
careful to pick around the nails,
this unpainting,
this stripping of the past owners'
marks was serious business,
the staircase,
the mantel,
all of these pieces
holding together the entry way
and Mom with that chandelier, god,
   the gurgly brown water
in the sink while you washed the crystal
that would clink together later
when I stomped the stairs or dad slammed the door,
this was the way that the sound of glass pinging
   came to represent
our differences, and me with the rainbow halo
from the front door peephole
as it lit the hallway to the kitchen wall,
all the way down, a beautiful mix of dust
and light, twirling, I used to dance
in the crossfire hoping to combust.

Love Is Water

Is it ingenious? An icicle as a murder weapon—
evidence that melts, maybe
it is the antidote to an ice queen,
a frozen staff, killing as some kind of homeopathy—
ice to ice equals blue flame and the smell
    of spent electricity,
or the smell of rain and just
a puddle of reflection—
like all those arty photos
of rivers reflecting trees and sky,
but more likely the puddle
would haunt me with my own
distracted icy eyes,
reflecting back the truth
of my own lack, a desert of thirst
for a love quench, lately
likened to the same quickly spent electricity.

Traveling the power lines
of a road familiar, farmland
stubbled with harvested carcasses
and puddles from the recent rain—
the hollows of uneven land.
The brown earth that I carved
out in imitation of the curves
of my favorite tromps.
They fill with falling rain
and those woman-made lakes
all add up to the whole body of you mother.

Acquisition vs. Creation

I come home for Christmas
to observe your religion,
equipped with wrapped gifts,
but my paper clashes with your décor.
Betting on last year's chromatic theme
of burgundy, mauve, and light pink,
I missed your memo of the move to greens.

Flashback to my arrival—
swathed in a pink baby blanket
from the agency—
I met my green room.

I set down my bag of presents
assuaged that "it's okay,"
because I "can place them at the back of the tree."
Paraded through the house past your family members,
met with hugs and the inspection
of the shortness of my hair,
the fluctuation of my weight,
all to see your new baskets—
the collection now over a hundred,
vicarious wombs everywhere—
the adopted daughter on display—
I am inundated by your obsession
when we reach the top of the stairs,
and I confront an altar to myself.
Twenty or so pictures perched on a chest of drawers
below the staircase window—
a rite of passage to second flight announcing
only those who accept your daughter
can pass to see
the immaculate bedrooms.

Porcelain

The painted face, delicate, thin, weightless
breaks in my white knuckled grip. I throw it
    against the wall
for emphasis.
This is what we've become—
silent rage exploding
into tangibles, collectible meaning broken,
    memories building
into tantrum shards that cut flesh,
a geneology of scars, to finger.
Great-grandmother's doll was within my reach
and the only thing to stop the yelling.
This is what we do—
change between the roles
mother, daughter, and monster as we collect
painted-up pretties to break
into pieces that we throw away.

The first morning breath came
as steam, I stepped over piles of wet leaves
crackling like cellophane
beneath my feet on Halloween.
Today, I stopped to finish my cigarette,
pivoted toward the street, looked up
through my billowing breath, exhaled smoke
to the skeleton that shed the leaves, and saw

an anarchy sign, fashioned
where birch limbs rose into a mercurial sky,
white veins slashed with black,
one twig broken into
a knotty curve converted
by the weather, conspiring to form the other three—
two slanted at opposites and one crossed
    in a malformed A,
like this was some sort of dream catcher
to chaos capture.

But that made no sense with recent events—
destruction, death's prevalence, and the ghosts
while the veil between worlds was at its thinnest—
instead, maybe it was a discriminating lens,
    a wooden window
for the power of planets, sun, and moon to focus in,
or maybe it was just the weather's jack-o-lantern,
    a ritual
carved to ward off evil
or say its own A-okay goodbye to Persephone.

She Was a Chagall

I was the Hulk, not green
but ugly and muscles, a transformation.
That night, I drank something nasty,
Jagermeister and Coke,
she called it sassafras, it was brown yuck
in a squat rocks glass. My face contorted,
and it slid to a clinking crash while
pretzel-like she showed me a yoga pose
called something I can't remember
but it looked to me like Kama-Sutra.
We brushed hands and torsos, trading turns
to the kitchen for more drinks.
I mocked her multi-vitamins, one-a-day,
her freezer filled with ginger root
and bagged kumquats.
When she laughed, she squinted and clapped.
I was a slave to her smile, tried to impress, I preyed on her
entertainment, my life a calendar marking days,
waiting for her legs, dancer-like to scissor open ooh—
and then after that night
for her paintings to include flying cows or chickens,
for her watercolor to bleed,
goldenrod to raspberry. She always wore
black socks and sandals, but it was somehow okay
because she could peel an orange
into the trash can and make it sexy.

Jam on the Exit Ramp

Cars flock off the map seeking gas or food
forming two lines around the flesh
of the mountain like your green pullover, unzipped,
circles your head. The two sides of a zipper split
circle my mind, and
I long to touch the cold edges of you,
prefer them, but I'm always the first car stopped
at the red light. Right now, a flashing four-way socks me
like the metaphor in your words:
The winter cap hanging on the coat-rack
at our diner looks like an unwrapped condom.
Coitus interruptus,
but ready, I rang the bell for assistance,
    paid our last check
Now I'm a lunatic honking my horn at traffic idiots,
    blowing a big
smacking pop from chewing gum bubble—
this was the wrong week to quit smoking.
I flip off the LeSabre in front of me:
"Fuck you grandpa." I survey my face in the rearview
for evidence of gum stuck, checking my time.
Damn watch battery preferring its own rhythms,
speeding up to slow down, making me late to leave you.
Now my radio is out of range, staticky,
so I pop in a tape and push play, but I'm on the
    wrong side,
so it spits back out, I flip it over and push in again,
    listening to
the lulling gravel of a voice dulled to a slow moving
    head nod
like rewind and exit lines that ooze
with the expediency and definition of grey.

I'm driving away from but closer to,
I rewind your one-sided tape
and listen over and again, mustering enough anger
at the truth in the lyrics—that you chose—to pick up
    my phone
and play part of our song to your voice mail
    accompanied by
"I'm really sorry it had to end in the middle like this."

She wanted to buy a dildo—a big, jelly, pink dong—
eight inches to strap on and thrust.
Her hips moved to meet her hands,
arms bent to illustrate faux fucking.
Boxing off my place within the gleam of her eyes,
her hips and arms—
how small and with purpose she had made me for.
Boxing me with an invisible dick,
air-slamming me with the force of an anger strumming
within her, like I was to be molded,
subsumed from her anger expelled, and I knew then
I should have run like hell,
but I feigned excitement, the experiment of toys.
Pretending to ignore the politics swarming
my head around the phallus, the addition to our sex,
I acquiesced, telling myself it would be different
than the   well the only thing I can remember
(I was almost always drunk)
was the pain hitting the back of my cervix,
with each thrust slow drumming
my body's rejection, clenched muscles traumatic,
I had hoped she would be more gentle,
but I knew her hands,
they were rough.
That evening the purchase loomed with obligation,
nagging my mind and reticent cunt
with every wink and eyebrow raise directed my way.
I really just wanted to go to sleep.
After-dinner TV droned, mixing with her laughter
and leg strokes until finally
I said, "How 'bout I try her on."

And I did. But this was no small task.
The cheap leather straps of a strap-on
are meant for women with no hips, no fat, small waists,
but I managed to get it on.
The side strap buckles cut into my puffy thighs,
and I thought about the chafing
of the pending consummation,
and then I looked in the mirror
and watched the dick bounce with my feet—
ball to heel to ball and back.
Then, I slapped it, and that was the best,
my own little punching bag.

I couldn't get over the humor,
but she found no comedy in it,
told me I was transferring my anxiety—
making fun because I was intimidated.
I continued my play,
took the dick out of the harness and twirled
my wrist, it followed my motion.
I joked about it as a weapon, and she'd had enough.
As she reached for it, I twirled; it hit her in the eye—
puffy and red it turned blue-black by morning.
She told everyone her shiner was from a "softball" incident.
I never stopped laughing.

I'm Not Bad with Directions

I know the red blinking light
means I should stop, turn here, leave
behind this pin-up pastiche,
this collecting of collisions
like croquet balls, fuck Britain.
I'd straighten my trajectory, my hammering
if I didn't enjoy
this shameless sacrament
not like any ordinary crisis.
This is my Church.
I feel the thrumming
the wooden apple in my chest,
I'm bleeding sweet.
I put the cut to my mouth and suck,
at some point I'm sure my mouth
will recognize the bitter pith and spit,
but the concaves will miss
and I like the curtains pulled back.
I want a better look at the corner.
I don't know which way to turn,
where to aim, this is the corner
where we crammed hours
into twenty minutes,
I'm stuck like Rothko
mixing perfect colors,
to capture the place—
the head lights, a halo, the sparkle
in rivulets of spittle,
between your mouth, my lips.
I was blind-sided,
what color was the ball
that you hit me with?

Whatever Returns, Returns to Find a Voice.

You traveled the path, pocketed the breadcrumbs
and met me, head in the oven, on the path back.
In our living room, the piano keys click down without fingers.
Whispering seeps from the corners,
creaking floors are the least of our worries.
To drown out the invisible heels,
we jump on the cracks, breaking my mother, my back—
story, but each one of those crumbs you've collected
were left by her, not me.

Cradling my weakness, you feed me vodka.
Drunk, I call you baby,
but I know you can't be possessed, because
you're not suffering because we touched.
That was a doozey of a line
the other night at the restaurant,
"you can touch my stuff," eyes dead on.
I knew exactly what you meant, but that is your way,
referring to the food, letting the double entendre dangle,
sprinkling invitation, intention all over the forked tasties
in front of my faces.

Later when you rubbed lotion
over my hands and arms
and we examined each others' skin, veins;
I fingered yours and flipped your hand to palm,
to trace your love line, looking for a way back
from this mess that is all mine.

Holding Weight

She hefted her story, all the heavy
and pressed the damage
into a box that split corners
when sat upon, the red pushed through
like her always cracked lips, or
her often self-inflicted wrists, the blood
she licked, metal, her impulse
was to suck at the flow.

The night before the last, she
stubbed her roach in my
ashtray and waited out
the song on the radio, bopping
her head and two yellowed-fingers along.

I thought of this, missed
while I waited the next night
for her to slam my trunk, take her shit
like the six shots of tequila.
Her foul mouth had stunk
up the bar yelling, slamming glasses
with a finishing thunk, sucking the lime pith
and with arm, wiping her salty lips. She was bold.
And she'd find a way in this world to take
it all and swallow hard
slamming glass
to show us all.
She was a fighter,
an assault on the eyes, ugly and beautiful,
but the constant mess of her
was too much even for my addictions.
I couldn't keep dancing, couldn't ignore

the pleasure she found in the perverts'
charades, the free drinks, the long stares
and "shake it over here's" that spun
a vortices of chaos,
a path. I wanted to hold down
and just love, but love could not break
her open. I knew it would be someone else's
bottle, a bar brawl or another
rape one day. She couldn't hold
still without the pain.

Like a praying mantis
she bent with both hands within
and said "it's like a little jelly bean,"
I asked, "does it hurt when you press on it?"
I thought of the list of bozos
she'd entertained in the past
year, thinking of sicko pics
out of a sex health book,
HPV looked like cauliflower dick.
I remembered the desperate 2 AM call on the
busted condom and the aborted little bastard
but she said,
"you don't have anything right?"

Stoned

You lit the match
for us both, sucked hard,
and started swinging
cigarette sparklers like fists.
Can't you just
hand me my fix? You're bad
as conductor. I should take
over, I'm tired of this wafting
stench, the smell of the crack
in our sanity. I was
the cracked white paint,
until you porched my tea,
took it with both hands away
from us on the swing,
matching rhythms
for nothing.

My legs like pipes, or streetlamps
that flicker off or on
with the ghosts I left for dead.
You remind me of no one.
You will always be
the camera I left in the wet basement,
It stopped working for me,
the last film not developed,
but full of snapshots that could twist
our lives up
worse than these shadows,
my dark, your light,
that keep us separate.

Unapologetically, you stole
my rings, the white dress,
only a few red spots,
I'll never know how easy on the thighs,
You wouldn't even kiss me on the mouth.
I'll always want you
coked up, mascara running
the sloppy mess of you
all over me, slurring the warble.
A warble of lies sounds like a fish out of water,
you are my walleye.

Just know
you'll be lit up
in my museum, my carved caution.
I'd call it love, but instead
wedge me a lime for my vodka, will you.
I've got 40 more before—
if this is
my mid-life crisis,
pass me another
mother's little helper
to get me through
until we're totally gone,
and just for the record,
tell me why
I'm your cove,
but I'll die alone, a captain
flagging the stone.

Geek

My knees went weak with the hobbit at the bar—
slicked back hair leather jacket greaser
but miniature and hump backed, I've got a sweet spot
for the freaks, my razor
sharp french fries cut
the roof of your mouth. I thought
about the blood in your mouth,
its metal sweet taste.
You are too close to not know
that now is the time of eggs,
my slip riding up, my grinding
against the chair, you must
remember the Cedar Point Demon Drop,
slow up, straight down fast,
like the funk music you like
to make love to. Dry ice
effects make me want a cigarette,
so that my smoke can fill your rooms,
though this is not Halloween,
it is your prom, like "Carrie"
but with conversational ooze covering me
like the bad northwestern habit
of ranch dressing with all things fried.
Your droopy smile is like a slide at the park
where I used to trim hedges, rusty with
chipped red paint, I miss happy hours of
halibut with tartar like home cooking.
I'll take your warm beer like a juice box
from a brown bagged lunch in the middle of summer,
but with a keg and plenty of red plastic cups.

Mirror, Mirror

Praying for myself, I think of you,
my only daughter,
don't worry, every body's ruined,
You were the belle before the ball. Come
home to me.
I have my old slipper
your foot will fit in.
Come home to me. Life,

can you forget?

I get so lonely in
the empty rooms,

I miss dressing you,
brushing the curls
I'm left with your childhood,
straight clumps,
an empty room.
Pink flowers,
and dolls displayed.
We don't touch china
faces, they break
open, empty,
losing their worth.

Do you remember the museum?
The carousel, the giraffe that you always rode?
The pennies that you threw into the wishing well.

Swimming in the deep end, do you remember, falling
off of the diving board? Or crashing the car?

Your poor broken pieces, I couldn't look.
Don't look down into the water,
your wishes will get reversed.

How Am I?

Licking salty tears from beat cheeks,
the outpour unused to,
like the blood,
like the socket incessantly tongued
from the tooth extracted,
this was one of those things
that you couldn't stop tasting or staring at,
its appall consumed
but eluded me.
As much as it pained
it sweetened, softened my thoughts,
made me kind.
Knowing my mother's fate,
it slowed me down,
made me think
of my own ways.

Funny, I can remember
I used to plead
to go to church on Sunday,
but we never made it, yet now
she begs me to go for her
like I have any clout
or desire to strike a deal
for her life,
if I believed in that
I'd be counting her diagnosis
as my own victory.
I almost wanted to thank her cancer.
But it is never that simple.
My expectation, waiting for approval and apology

were stripped, a sort of relief, but my body is left holding
the memories' weight,
the way you feel when
you've removed rollerskates,
replaced shoes,
or swung a lead bat
before an aluminum.
The sudden lightness propels you
into a way off balance.

I don't know if I can really feel,
it is more like ideas about feeling
float out of me
like globules of mercury
rolling around on the tile floor
stopping in the cracks
to assume their shape,
but what are they
but like something else?

—ode to a vegetarian girlfriend

I hesitate to order meat, but I want it.
The chewing of flesh,
chicken body, muscles, sinew,
a tough bird.
My mind fights first with her
ideologies then with the snapshots of what I know—
the unclean coop, cages, the butchering
and suddenly I'm tracing backward
the fate of an animal, this bird
until I'm transfixed by the grotesque
nature of a murderous need—unable to swallow.
man's war with beast, each bite contrition
to her and the life of a chicken
I never heard squawk,
I want to give it back the privilege of flight.

My mind is all feathers, feet like twigs, feed scattered in mud.
Mr. Darwin tell me, am I fit
to take these things in my mouth?
Is this survival or domination. I argue protein, but sure
I could eat some beans.
I see how to her these murderous acts are a carnival of macabre.
But I enjoy the taste, and tell me where does pleasure fit.

And then the girl, when I take her in—how does that fit.
I've no dick to dominate, to pummel her with, nor she I,
but I know that she is mine when
I have her clit between my teeth,
my tongue licking the juice of her meats' release.
This eating out, how does this fit?
And if it does, what chain do I weaken, what link releases?

Word Tryst

God, I miss the smell of your cologne like citrus vodka—
I miss licking it off of your neck. Some kind of body shot.
Your sex was always an assault
like the pigeon that ransacked
your rainy-day beach date with the bracelet girl.
Too bad you got a splinter in your ass from the bench
and then pigeon shit in your hair.
But I appreciate your candor; you still have no game.
I miss your golf umbrella on wet days like this.
I wish I could bring you a bouquet of stinky daisies
and sing you hip-hop opera, but
I don't know what the fuck that is,
but I could make a mean drum beat
with my mouth while you freestyle some html,
it'd make everything better,
our nonsense always did, and then
I could take you
to the arcade and we could play
ski ball. I could wear the hot plaid pants
that go so well with your red shirt,
and don't ask, because I'm not giving it back.
I would offer you shelter from the rain, but
we promised to move on and I don't want
your jelly bracelet girl
to get mad and melt wax on her arms
like that is cryptic.

She Is Voodoo, I'm the Doll

I had to cut the tag in my t-shirt,
it reminded me of her nails on my back.

She sent a card, offered condolences,
        but none she was ready to give.
Maybe coffee, a conversation, some sweet
forked confections,
but no tears, or grief.
An epicurean, everything was about her.
The card decorum. Icing. Lace.
The pretty things girls are made of.
It had nothing to do with how she felt,
and it certainly wasn't an invitation.
I was her kewpie doll, chubby cheeks and curly hair.
She was old enough to be my mother,
        but of the privileged
taxonomy and my time was a voucher for free
lunch, dinner, drinks when she felt like charity.
I didn't kowtow, but I was quiet a lot.
Let her talk. Listened, genuinely, but the closer we got,
        the more I felt
she was shaving my edges, a lathe.
I lost my flicker, my bounce, she'd stolen my indignation.
I became conduit for fake,
passed it on like an epidemic. It was ennui, entropy,
my Pluto in retrograde. I thought the hubbub
        that followed her
was unreal, made-up ego, but everyone I met knew her.
        Weird.
She was scratching my surfaces long after our last
        cup of coffee.